A Glory Filled Future

Understanding end-time events and the marriage connection

JOHN E JOHANSSON

A Glory Filled Future

Understanding end-time events and the marriage connection

By John E. Johansson
Edited by Philip Severi

Published by Shophar Publishing
PO Box 2124
Deming, NM. 88031

This book or parts thereof may not be reproduced in any form, stored in a retrieval system, or transmitted in any form by any means – electronic, mechanical, photocopy, recording, or otherwise – without prior written permission of the publisher, except as provided by United States of America copyright law.

ISBN-10: 0-9992833-0-8
ISBN-13: 978-0-9992833-0-1

Copyright © 2017 by John Johansson

Scripture taken from the New King James Version®. Copyright © 1982 by Thomas Nelson, Inc. Used by permission. All rights reserved.

Copyright © 2017 by John E. Johansson

I have known this author for the past twenty-five years or more. I have known John to be a student of the Word of God. He is a man that lives out the convictions of his heart.

As I read this manuscript, I am reminded of a country song recorded by country artist, Garth Brooks. The song: "If tomorrow never comes". Brooks sings about his wife and her knowing how much he truly loves her. John brings out what a genuine relationship with Jesus Christ produces. Love. Being prepared to actually meet Jesus, if tomorrow never comes. True in marriage and true in life, we are the Bride of Christ preparing for our wedding.

As you read the book you now hold in your hands, allow the Word of God to penetrate your heart, to search the hidden chambers and reveal everything needed for you to be truly ready for the wedding.

Let us rejoice and be glad and give him glory! For the wedding of the Lamb has come, and his bride has made herself ready.
Rev. 19:7 (NIV)

Pastor Tom Smith
Marriage and Family Pastor
The House Church, Modesto, Ca.

****

John's study of ancient Jewish wedding customs brings fresh and challenging insights into the many scriptures relating to end times.

You will find yourself reading passages that John cites and asking the Holy Spirit for still more insight and wisdom; always a good reaction.

Ken Swett, Pastor
Modesto Foursquare Church

Table of Contents

Preface

A Key

The Key Explained

Jesus, Our Groom

The Church, His Bride

Anticipation of the Bride

Preparation of the Bride

The Great Divorce

The Groom Returns

A Sobering Thought

At the Father's House

The Grand Appearing

What's the Point?

Preface

The date was March 29, 1980, a day that I believe would forever change the course of my life. As a young teenager growing up in church and in a Christian home, I heard people talk of Jesus. I saw many respond to alter calls, asking Jesus into their lives. But it was on this date, kneeling beside my bed, that my dad led me to Jesus. I often go back to that night, wondering how my life would have been different if I hadn't responded to God's tug on my heart, a tugging that seemed to last for several months. My mom tells me that I gave my life to Jesus when I was five years old, but sadly, that is an event I don't remember. It was on that premise God began to draw me into a relationship with Him during my teenage years. Up to that time I had plans for my life, and for the most part God wasn't in them, except in a casual way that would be characterized by church attendance and Bible reading.

Leading up to that night beside my bed, more than thirty-five years ago, I remember situations and experiences in which it was evident God's protective hand was present. But it was also in those same situations God made one thing clear to me: if I had died at any time I would not have gone to heaven. At the same time, I was also keenly aware that if the Rapture were to take place I could possibly be left behind. I feared that possibility because I knew how bad things would get during the Tribulation period that followed. After that night, the night I finally surrendered my life to Jesus, I became excited about end-time events. I knew the fulfillment of these Biblically prophesied events only pointed to a glorious future with Jesus in heaven that was getting so much closer to fulfillment.

Over the years, my interest in end-time events has only grown. Along with that increasing interest has been a growing concern for Christians who are not taking their relationship with Jesus seriously, instead treating it casually or non-chalantly. For more than twenty-five years my heart has been concerned for these casual Christians, challenging them in their walk with Christ, and the eternity that awaits them. One of the reasons I've found some to be so casual in their relationship with Christ is that they are not convinced He is returning any time soon. Others might not want Him to return because life is too good for them right now. Maybe they do not fully understand that there is a glory filled future that awaits followers of Christ, or that the entrance to that future is right around the corner through an event known as the Rapture.

We're living in a time when the world in general is feeling more despair for the future than ever before. The world sees things falling apart in so many ways, afraid also of an apocalyptic disaster of some sort about to hit and change life as we know it. As for the church in general, more and more Christians are embracing the idea that there is no Rapture for the Church, or if there is, it won't be anytime soon. Many others are more concerned about building what I call a kind of Christian utopia more than they are in reaching the lost with the Gospel and the hope and assurance of a glory filled future in heaven that it brings.

With this book, it is my hope that you will be assured of the glory filled future that awaits followers of Christ. It is a hope that transcends the despair and hopelessness that seems to be growing each day. Solid, eternal, and beyond imagination is the hope found in relationship with Jesus alone. No person, no government, no policy or law, no amount of money, no activity, or anything else can give you this solid, promising hope for the future like Jesus does. Yet more and more people, even within church circles, are looking for such a hope outside of Jesus. This book is designed to give you the tools and understanding to embrace the hope found in Christ for yourself. If your hope is not grounded and planted firmly in Christ, may this book help you find it in Him.

A Key

Bible prophecy and end-time events. A subject that has captivated the hearts and minds of many over the centuries, both Christians and non-Christians alike. We live with the wonder of what the future has in store for us, whether it be positive or not. Some envision a future of great technological advancements that make life easier and more comfortable for all, as well as expanding life as we know it well beyond the confines of this planet we call Earth. For others, they see nothing but very dark and apocalyptic times coming, a period when just about any scenario you can imagine can become reality, including the potential end of all humanity. As crazy as things are in the world we live in, many are wondering where it's all going to end up, and if it's even going to be something to which we should be looking forward. Anticipating worst case scenarios, many have gone to great lengths to prepare themselves for what they think will come. They hope to outlive and survive these worst-case scenarios to a time when we will have risen above them.

When we look at Bible prophecy, we know that what awaits us is both the most glorious and exciting of times, as well as the scariest of all circumstances we can imagine. What determines our perspective of Bible prophecy, and what it says awaits us, hinges upon our relationship with Christ, if we even have one. If we are Christians, then what awaits us is a life in eternity far greater and glorious than we can ever imagine. But for those who are not Christians, the Bible clearly tells us that the worst of what can be imagined awaits them for all eternity. It is only avoidable if you give your life to Jesus before that happens.

Within church circles, there are many different views and opinions regarding Bible prophecy and end-time events. The reasons for many of these differing views are due to a lack of Biblical understanding and how to interpret Bible prophecy accurately. While some views are strongly supported by Scripture, others are not. Still others attempt to support their views Scripturally by twisting or taking out of context various passages in the Bible.

God gives us many clues throughout the Bible of what is to be expected in the end-times. We have an image from Nebuchadnezzar's dream that symbolizes the different kingdoms, or empires, that would rule at different times. We have Daniel telling us of the seventy weeks God is using to deal with Israel, which includes the last week we identify as the Tribulation period. In that same passage in Daniel, we also read of the one that we recognize as the anti-Christ. Ezekiel speaks of a great war that is to come against Israel, and the different armies that will be involved with it. Jesus gives us some of the signs evident in the last days, signs both on earth and in the heavens. The Apostle Peter said there would be scoffers in the last days, scoffing at the idea of Jesus returning. The Apostle Paul wrote about the Rapture of the Church. These are just some of the clues that we're given about the end-times, but even with all the clues we're given in Scripture it is sometimes hard to wrap our head around what is to come. To understand the significance of the clues and how they fit in Bible prophecy and end-time events, we need a key.

When we talk of keys to understanding Bible prophecy regarding the end-times, there are three that come to mind. The first one is found in the seven feasts God instituted for Himself in Leviticus 23. In the feasts, we see God's plan for the redemption of mankind and the restoration of God's kingdom on earth. The first three feasts were already fulfilled in order with Jesus' death, burial, and resurrection, and the fourth feast was fulfilled later with the birth of the Church on the Day of Pentecost. The remaining three feasts point to the Rapture of the church, the judgments and conclusion of the Tribulation period, and the millennial reign of

Christ.

The second key that comes to mind is centered around three harvests mentioned in Scripture, the barley, the wheat, and the grape harvests. The barley harvest represents those caught up and resurrected at the Rapture, the wheat represents those resurrected as martyrs for Christ in the Tribulation period, and the grape harvest represents those at the end of the Tribulation period. When you look a bit deeper, even the different phases associated with the harvests can be seen in Bible prophecy.

In this book, I want to share and focus on the third key, a key that screams out to us from Genesis through Revelation. It's a key that is rarely mentioned with end-time events, but it's a vital key in understanding much of what is ahead for us. When we look at this key God has given us, it will do more than just help us understand Bible prophecy, it will also challenge us to re-evaluate some of the theological teachings we've embraced and held onto considering Scripture.

The key that I want to share with you is what I call, the marriage connection. Outside of the fact that Christians make up the Bride of Christ, it's rare that you will hear marriage and end-time events mentioned in the same conversation. It hasn't been until the past several years that people have begun to recognize the connection between Bible prophecy and marriage, but even with that recognition, most still are not aware of the relationship. As we begin to dig into this you will find that marriage is strongly and solidly connected to end-time events within Scripture.

The Key Explained

To understand Bible prophecy, it's important for us to know and understand the keys God has given us to aid us in that understanding. Marriage is one of those keys. While it may sound rather odd to think that marriage could be one of the keys to understanding end-time events, as you will see, it is one of the biggest keys needed.

To view end-time events in light of the marriage key, it is important for us to examine it more closely. When we read of marriage in the Scriptures, there is a tendency to view it from the eyes of American culture. By doing so we get an inaccurate picture of what marriage means from a Biblical perspective. Even our own relationship with Christ is negatively influenced by our understanding of marriage from what we know it to be here in America.

Many times, when we look at marriage and what it means, we will usually look at what the Apostle Paul writes in Ephesians 5. This is a good thing in that it gives us a model, a picture, of what marriage should look like, but if we stop there our understanding of what Paul is trying to tell us begins to break down. Paul tells us that the relationship between a husband and wife is a picture the relationship between Christ and the Church. But if we stop at this point our understanding of both relationships remains incomplete. The reason for this is because we don't understand the example of marriage at which the Apostle Paul was looking.

Paul wasn't seeing America's version of marriage simply because it would be another 1700+ years before America would be formed. Instead he was seeing marriage from the viewpoint of the Jews and their marriage customs. Some would argue against viewing marriage through the Jewish culture of Paul's day, maintaining that it doesn't really matter since it wasn't a perfect example to follow. However, as imperfect as it may or may not have been, we must acknowledge that Paul's vision of marriage came through the culture in which he was raised. Therefore, the parallels between the Jewish view of marriage and Christ's relationship with the Church remain strikingly similar in many ways.

To begin with, in the marriage customs of Paul's day, the groom would identify whom he would like to have as his wife. Then he would seek his father's approval. If his father approved, the groom and his father would approach the potential bride and her family, bringing various gifts and tokens with them for her. If the potential bride indicates an interest in becoming this man's wife, the groom would then present her with a Ketubah, a legally binding contract identifying various ways he would provide for her in the marriage, or afterwards if at any time the marriage is broken through death or divorce. If the potential bride accepts the groom's proposal and Ketubah, they would then seal the arrangement. Sometimes this would be done by drinking from the same cup, showing that they were entering a marriage contract with each other. This also signified the start of the betrothal period.

Once the bride and groom entered this marriage contract, the groom would then leave her to go prepare a place for her at his father's house. When the groom left to prepare a place for his bride, they would not consummate, or in other words finalize, the marriage contract until he returned for her at a time neither one of them knew. Generally, this period lasted about a year, but it could be sooner or later depending on how things went. In either case, the groom had to wait for his father to give him the "go ahead" before he could return for her. Per Jewish law, the bride and groom in the betrothal stage were considered, for all intents and purposes, as married. Therefore, the consequences of being unfaithful to each other was very severe, as if the marriage had already been finalized.

So, what is with this betrothal period? For one thing, betrothal is very different than the practice of engagement here in America. The definition of betrothal according to the Merriam-Webster online dictionary is:

1) the act of betrothing or fact of being betrothed,

2) a mutual promise or contract for a future marriage.

To be betrothed to another was not something to be taken lightly, the consequences of being unfaithful to the other party being severe. When the bride accepted the groom's proposal of marriage the two entered a legal contract that was recognized and enforced civilly, religiously, and socially. In America, to be engaged is nothing more than the mutual consent by both parties to get married at a future time, something that could easily be canceled at the discretion of either of them in the simplest of ways. With an engagement, there is no legal, contractual arrangement in place, and there are no legal or financial consequences for unfaithfulness. Unlike engagement that can be canceled just by saying so, the only way to cancel or break a betrothal was by death or divorce. To view betrothal in the same way we view engagement is misleading, causing us to misstate where we are in our relationship with Christ.

When it came time for the father to give his son the "go ahead" to return for his bride, the groom would return for her with little or no warning. During this betrothal period, it was expected of the bride to: 1) prepare herself for his return, and 2) be watching for him since she didn't know when he would come for her.

When the groom returns for his bride, he takes her back to his father's house. There they will consummate and finalize the marriage contract between them, the start of living together for life.

Before continuing, a question must be asked. Did the groom always take his bride back to his father's house when he returns for her? Sadly, no, this wasn't the case. If the groom returned and found that his bride had either been unfaithful to him by having her affections elsewhere, or had not been watching and properly preparing herself for his return, he could return to his father's house without her and subsequently give her a letter of divorce. This is also a part of the key found in marriage to help us understand end-time events and our relationship with Christ.

Shall we continue? When the groom and bride return to the father's house they enter under the huppah (hoopah) where the wedding ceremony takes place.

They are then ushered into the bridal chamber where they consummate the marriage. This kicks off the marriage feast that generally lasted about a week, or seven days. During this time of feasting friends, family, and guests of the family come and go, taking part in their time of celebration.

After the festivities, the bride and groom together leave his father's house to be seen publicly by the community for the first time since the wedding. Where they had previously been identified as bride and groom, they are now identified as husband and wife. While their preparations for marriage kept them apart for about a year, it is now that they begin their life together as one, and to be seen together in public lets everyone else know that their new life together has officially begun.

You may already see the connection between Biblically prophesied end-time events and Biblical marriage, but if not, that is okay. We will go more in-depth with this in the following chapters. As we look more into this, it will become more evident that we need to view end-time events through the eyes of the Ancient Jewish marriage customs, and less through the eyes of our American culture.

Jesus, Our Groom

To see the relevance of marriage to end-time events, it's important that we see Jesus as our Groom. The Apostle Paul, in Ephesians 5:22-33, connected our relationship to Christ with that of marriage between one man and one woman. In this passage, Paul tells us that husbands represent Christ, and that wives represent the Church. This means that Jesus is the Church's Groom. The Apostle Paul goes on to say in 2 Corinthians 11:2 that we are in fact betrothed to Jesus. While both passages make it clear that Jesus is our Groom, these alone do not show the connection between end-time events and marriage that we want to cover in this book. In the previous chapter, we looked at the marriage customs of the ancient Jews, and in this chapter, we're going to see how Jesus fills the role of the groom in that context.

The marriage between Jesus and the Church began when Jesus chose us as His Bride. We didn't choose Him, but Jesus tells us in John 15:16 that He chose us. It is at this point that He presented us with a Ketuba, a contract customarily given to the bride-to-be, outlining what the groom will provide for the bride. The bride-to-be in the ancient Jewish marriage customs had to decide after reviewing the marriage contract she'd been presented with, whether she is willing to accept what this man is proposing to her or not. It's called, counting the cost

The ketuba Jesus gives us is a bit different than what grooms traditionally gave the bride-to-be. However, we as the bride must still fulfill this ancient custom. In Luke 14:25-34, Jesus tells us that we need to count the cost of following Him, and that not doing so could lead to failure and embarrassment for us. Jesus gives us His ketuba, the Bible and His teachings, so it is up to us to decide if it's worth it to us to agree to His terms and to follow Him.

Sadly, the need for such consideration is one aspect that is quickly disappearing from what is being preached and taught from pulpits within church circles. It's one thing to look at the benefits of following Jesus, of which there are many, including those that are eternal. But if we fail to identify and share what the cost of following Jesus looks like, then the gospel we're sharing with people is incomplete. This must be emphasized! Jesus tells us in Luke 14 that we need to count the cost to follow Him, and He gives us some serious things to consider. If we ignore them and only focus on the blessings and positives of following Him, merely by acknowledging who He is and what He's done for us, we are not representing Him as we ought and are "selling" people a gospel that conflicts with the true Gospel of Christ.

Once we agree to the terms of this relationship Christ offers us, we have entered the betrothal stage of our marriage to Him. In ancient times, it was not uncommon for the groom and bride to drink from the same cup at this point as a way of officially sealing their commitment to each other. It has been suggested by some that this betrothal cup is represented by the cup we drink from in communion.

Some of the gifts that the groom gave his new bride were tokens that would identify her in the sight of others as "spoken for" and belonging to someone. The Apostle Paul, in 2 Corinthians 11:2, tells us that we are betrothed to Christ. One of the gifts that mark us in a similar way can be found in the presence of the Holy Spirit, much like an engagement ring in American culture. Paul tells us in Ephesians 1:13-14 that after we heard the gospel and placed our trust in it, we were then sealed by the Holy Spirit until our redemption is made complete. In 2 Corinthians 1:21-22, Paul also tells us that God has given us the Holy Spirit as a guarantee, or in some translations, a deposit, until the time that our redemption is completed.

Once the groom and his new bride entered the betrothal stage of their marriage, it was now time for the groom to depart to prepare a place for his bride. The groom would leave his bride to prepare a place for her in his father's house, a process that could take as long as a year on average. In John 14:1-3, Jesus begins by telling us not to let our hearts be troubled, something I could imagine a groom would say to assure his new bride that he would be returning for her. Jesus then tells us that He's going to His Father's house to prepare a place for us, and that He would be returning for us so we could be with Him. When the groom left to prepare a place for his new bride, he didn't know when he would be returning as that decision was left to his father to decide. Speaking of when He would be returning for us, Jesus tells in Matthew 24:36 and Mark 13:32 that no one knows when that time will be, not Him, not the angels in heaven, but only the Father. Can you see how closely the Jewish marriage customs compare with the relationship Jesus was describing between Him and us?

Since the groom didn't know when he would be returning, the bride had no idea as to when to expect him. It was up to her to keep watching for him. Similarly, in Luke 21:34-36, Mark 13:32-33, and Matthew 25:1-13, Jesus tells us to be watching for His return. He doesn't tell us to do so in the form of a suggestion, or that it would be wise for us to do. Instead, He strongly commands us to do so, as though a lot is hinging on it. This is exactly what a groom would be telling his new bride to be doing. Jesus is coming back for us, probably much sooner than most care to acknowledge or admit, so it is imperative that we heed His command to be watching for Him.

When we talk of weddings and all the work there is in preparing for them, often there is that one person who will do what she or he can to help the bride prepare herself for that special day. Perhaps it's her mom or a close friend or relative, but sometimes it's someone that has been hired for that one task. Jesus sent someone with that one task in mind, to prepare us for when He does return to receive us to Himself. Jesus tells us in John 16:7-15 that He was going to send the Holy Spirit, the Helper, the one that will lead us into all truth, pointing everyone to Jesus. The Holy Spirit, our wedding planner you can say, has been given to us to help us prepare for Christ's return. The reason for this is simple. The Apostle Paul, in Ephesians 5:26-27, tells us that Jesus is returning for a bride without spot or wrinkle. This would imply that the Bride has a responsibility during this betrothal stage, that she is to take the time that He is away to prepare Herself for Him. It is the Holy Spirit who helps us with that. The above passage also implies that we need to be diligent to not let life or the mindsets and things of this world to keep us from being ready when He does return for us.

When the groom's father gave the word, the groom would immediately go to receive his bride. He would go with little to no warning to get her, after which they would head back to the father's house for the marriage feast and the consummation of the marriage covenant between them. Just like in ancient times, when the Father gives Jesus the word that all is ready, Jesus will immediately come for His Bride. Jesus is returning to receive unto Himself His Bride, the Church, an event we refer to as the Rapture. This is a major, Biblically prophesied end-times event that has yet to be fulfilled and is closely connected with our marriage relationship with Christ. We're told in 1 Thessalonians 4:13-18 that Jesus is coming back for us and that we will be caught up, raptured physically to meet Jesus in the air on our way to meet the Father and the wedding ceremony. We're also told in 1 Corinthians 15:50-58 that there will be a physical transformation which we will experience at that moment. I don't know about you, but I'm excited about, and looking forward to, that moment that is just over the horizon, when we will be caught up to be with our Lord forever.

The Apostle Paul tells us in Ephesians 5:26-27 that

Jesus is looking to receive unto Himself a glorious church, one without spot or wrinkle, holy and without blemish. This is one of the reasons the Holy Spirit has been sent to us, why we've been given God's Word, the Bible, that we may be prepared for Jesus when He returns. This passage implies there is a process in place by which we become the glorious church He's coming back for, and we'll cover that more in another chapter. But the fact remains that He's coming back with some expectations of His Bride.

It will be a major event when Jesus returns for us, His Bride. Paul gives us an idea of what to expect at that time in two passages, 1 Thessalonians 4:13-18 and 1 Corinthians 15:50-58. We read in Thessalonians that there's going to be a lot of noise when this happens; Jesus will descend from heaven with a shout, the voice of an archangel, along with the trumpet of God. With that noise, we also read that those who are dead will be raised up to meet Christ in the air, and then those of us who are alive and remain in Christ will be caught up to meet Jesus. In Corinthians, we read that in a moment, in the twinkling of an eye, at the last trump we will all be changed. At that moment, the bodies we now have that are in continuous decay and corruption will be changed, putting on incorruption and immortality. Isn't that exciting? Perhaps you're dealing with constant and severe aches and pains, or some form of dismemberment or disability, but at that moment those things will all be gone as your body will be changed into something glorious. What a moment that will be to behold!

According to the ancient Jewish marriage customs, after the groom came to receive his bride to himself, the two of them would return to his father's house where they would consummate the marriage and have a week-long marriage feast. When Jesus returns for His bride, He is not coming to establish His kingdom here on earth at that time, but instead to take us back to His Father's house where our marriage relationship with Him will be completed and finalized.

But for some such a completion will never happen. In both Mark 8:38 and Luke 9:26, Jesus tells us that those in this sinful and adulterous generation who are ashamed of Him and His words when He returns in His glory, the glory of the Father and with the holy angels, He will likewise be ashamed of them before the Father and the holy angels. This tells us two things: 1) we cannot be ashamed to honor and proclaim Him with our life and words, and 2) if we are ashamed of Him and His words, then He's going to be ashamed to even introduce or present us to the Father at the wedding. This is perhaps one of the reasons some who claim to be Christians will be left behind when Jesus returns for His bride. We'll cover this more in a later chapter.

As we can see, Jesus is not only a groom, but He's our groom. There are some who want to say that the Church is not the Bride of Christ, some even thinking that the bride is the New Jerusalem. However, in

Scripture we only see Jesus filling the role of a groom to only one "person", and that is the Church. The things Jesus said, and the description of events yet to come given to us by the Apostles, both resemble ancient Jewish marriage customs and point to the Church as being the Bride of Christ. There is nothing more glorious for men and women to look forward to than the glory filled future that awaits them in eternity as the bride and wife of Jesus.

The Church, His Bride

We saw how Jesus fulfills the role of groom in our relationship with Him. In this chapter, we're going to look at how the Church fulfills the role of bride in that same relationship with Jesus. In doing so, we need to remember that Jesus first chose us to be His Bride, not the other way around. We're told in 1 John 4:19 that He loved us first. The extent of that love for us is emphasized in Romans 5:8 when it tells us that while we were yet sinners, He died for us. Not only did Jesus first love us when we weren't loveable, while we were still sinners, but also that His love for us was so great that He willingly and voluntarily died in our place so He could have a relationship with us. We're told in 1 John 4:8 that God is love, and we see the greatness of His love for us in that He died for us.

So, where does that leave us? Jesus tells us in John 3:16, probably the most popular Scripture passage known by Christians and non-Christians alike, that all who believe in Him would have eternal life. Now the belief Jesus is referring to is more than just mentally believing in who Jesus is and in what He did for us. Instead, it is a belief that takes that knowledge and translates it into the way people live their lives. Romans 10:9-10 lets us know how such a surrendered life begins. It starts by believing with the heart, not just the mind, that God has raised Jesus from the dead, then confessing with our mouth that Jesus is Lord. This is the point at which we enter this relationship with Christ. In 2 Corinthians 11:2, the Apostle Paul lays out precisely this beginning, letting us know that we are betrothed to Jesus. Romans 7:4 reinforces this thought when the Apostle Paul further states, remembering that it is through salvation as we've just seen that we become dead to the law, that through the body of Christ of which we become a part, we may be married to Him, Jesus.

Earlier we saw that the groom would present to his potential bride a ketubah, a legally binding contract that guaranteed the bride certain protections and rights, especially in the event of a divorce. Jesus gives us a ketubah in the form of the Bible, but the ketubah He presents to us is a little different from the traditional ketubah associated with ancient Jewish marriage customs. In His ketubah, not only does Jesus give us various gifts and promises, but He also puts some responsibility on His Bride if she is to possess all of them, including eternal life. In this ketubah we call the Bible, Jesus makes it clear that His commitment and faithfulness to us is very solid and assured, that He will never leave us or forsake us. But does He lay any responsibility for this relationship we have with Him at our own feet? Some take the position that once they enter this relationship with Christ, there is nothing more for them to do. It is true that Ephesians 2:8-9 tells us salvation is by grace and through faith, and that there is nothing we could do to earn or obtain it. But does that mean we have no responsibility for how we live once we've entered this relationship? As we continue it will become evident that we do have a responsibility regarding what we do with this new life we've gained through faith in Christ.

We already covered in a previous chapter that it is important for us to count the cost of following Jesus. In this chapter, we're going to take a closer look at what it means to be not just a follower of Christ, but also to be the Bride of Christ. In Luke 9:23-25, Jesus tells us what is expected of those who follow Him. Following Jesus is not for the faint of heart since it requires that people count the cost of following Him. Some may argue that they entered a marriage relationship with Christ based on grace and faith, and that any hint of them needing to do anything more than that is purely legalistic in nature, but is it? The focus of this book, in addition to showing the connection between major Biblical end-time events and marriage, is to show how our salvation by grace is different from our life as one betrothed to Christ. In Matthew 7:13-14, Jesus tells us that the gate is wide and the way is broad that leads to destruction, but He also tells us that narrow is the gate and difficult the way that leads to eternal life, and only a few find it. It's easy to get through the gate to destruction, but it's a difficult road to travel the road to eternal life. To enter the marriage covenant and betrothal with Jesus is a relatively easy thing to do. But it is in counting the cost of following Jesus that each person determines whether eternal life is worth traveling the difficult road to get there or not.

Once the bride and groom formally entered a marriage covenant with each other, the groom would immediately leave the bride to go prepare a place at his father's house for his new bride. They had entered a marriage covenant, but their marriage would not be finalized until after the groom returned for her, taking her back to his father's house to consummate, to make final, their marriage. The bride did not know when her groom would return for her, and sometimes she would have to wait more than 12 months for him. During this time, it was up to her to keep watching for him. The bride's diligence in keeping watch for her groom showed that her heart's desire was for him. It was important for the groom to see this, as we will further learn in a later chapter.

On multiple occasions Jesus told His followers to watch and pray regarding His return for them. I've heard Christians indicate that there is no need for them to be watching for Him, taking the position that when He returns they will automatically be taken up, raptured, to meet Him in the air. Others have said that living the Christian life is watching for Him, so to be actively watching for Him is unnecessary. Many dismiss or discount Jesus' commands to us to watch and pray, but His words to us are in the context of the marriage terms from Him to His Bride, the Church. I don't know what would be said between a groom and his bride before he left to prepare a place for her, but it was clear that she was to be keeping watch for his eventual return for her.

That context shows that, like her, it is our responsibility as His Bride to be watching for Him to return for us. This is one of the responsibilities of the bride, and it is one of the responsibilities for all those who enter a marriage covenant with Christ through salvation.

While the bride waited for the return of her groom, she would change her appearance. What she then wore was a sign that she was spoken for and already betrothed to someone. This might also include wearing some of the jewelry she received from her groom when they entered the betrothal stage. What she was doing in changing her appearance was letting others know that she was exclusively someone else's bride and was now unavailable to others. Similarly, as Christians, as the Bride of Christ, we are told to be set apart for Him, to be sanctified and holy. In 1 Peter 1:15-16, the Apostle Peter reminds us that we are to be holy as God is holy. Our thoughts, our conduct and the way we live, and even our speech needs to be holy and set apart to Him as He is. Our thoughts should no longer resemble the thoughts and mindsets of the world, but instead resemble and reflect to the world around us what God's Word says to us. Our conduct and lifestyle shouldn't resemble that of the world and how the world says we ought to live, but instead should represent and reflect the nature and heart of God as revealed in His Word. Our speech and the way we talk shouldn't reflect or sound the same as the world, but rather be in line with what we see in God's Word. Our attitudes, our motivations, and our priorities in life should not resemble those of the world, but should instead represent a life changed and set apart for God and His purposes. In Romans 12:1-2 we're told to not be conformed to this world, but to be transformed by the renewing of our minds. We're told in Philippians 4:8 how we should think, or rather what our thoughts should focus on, which is different from the way the world thinks. We're told in Proverbs 23:7 that a man is according to his thoughts. Finally, Jesus said in Luke 6:45 that out of the abundance of the heart the mouth speaks. Everything about our lives should reflect to others that our lives are not our own, but rather God's, to be set apart for Him and used as He sees fit to use them.

In John 13:34-35, Jesus tells us that we are to love one another, and it will be in this that people will know that we are His disciples. This is another way in which we show that we are set apart to Him, and not to another.

While this reference in John describes our love for each other, how does Jesus know that we love Him? Some say that He's God, and that He just knows because He knows everything. Others say He knows we love Him based on our love for one another as we previously stated, but is that true? While at the same time others will know if we are His disciples by our love for one another, the standard by which Jesus determines if we love Him is different. John 14:15-31 tells us that Jesus will know if we love Him if we keep and obey His commands. In the same way, many times in 1 John we're told that God knows if we love Him if we obey

His commandments, and we know if we love God if we obey His commandments. Therefore, while we wait for the return of Christ for us, His Bride, we need to demonstrate our love for Him by being obedient to all His commands for us.

Everything discussed in this chapter points to one thing. In Ephesians 5:26-27 we're told that Christ is coming back for a Bride without spot or wrinkle. What we do while we wait for Him, what we've previously read, works to prepare us as a Bride without spot or wrinkle when He returns for us. This doesn't mean that we will have "obtained" by the time He arrives. But I do believe if our hearts are right, and we're actively being transformed as we read in Romans 12:2, striving to make ourselves presentable to Him and free of sin in our own life, then His grace will cover those areas where we fall short. Jesus returning for His Bride is a fulfillment of a major prophetic end-times event we identify as the Rapture, an event you don't want to miss because of any negligence on your part to prepare for properly.

Anticipation of the Bride

When a man and a woman agree to marry each other, they are both eagerly looking forward to that day. For a man, it is often an anticipation not so much of the ceremony as it is with what will later follow on that day between the two of them alone. Yes, he is looking forward to spending the rest of his life with his bride, but the growing anticipation he's usually looking forward to is the ultimate in physical intimacy they will enjoy later that same day. The bride, however, is looking more to the ceremony and what it represents: the start of a new life exclusive to the two of them and their commitment to each other alone. It is the bride's anticipation that I want to focus on in this chapter, which is a picture of the anticipation the Church should have regarding its marriage to Jesus.

Over the years, I have noticed something about the bride's excitement and anticipation of her wedding day. I've heard non-stop talk about the groom, sometimes to the point that even her girlfriends become sick and tired of hearing talk about him all the time. I remember hearing of one bride who had gone for a day of shopping with her girlfriends a couple hundred miles away. She kept wondering and asking the other girls if her groom would like one outfit or another on her or not. Some are counting down the days, and with each day they get closer to the wedding day their excitement only grows. Their lives and their thoughts are almost entirely centered on their groom and their upcoming wedding day. Often, they will have a starry-eyed expression on their faces, a glow of sorts that sometimes makes them stand out in a crowd. They can't seem to get enough of their groom, always eager to talk and spend time with him. I've even seen how their growing anticipation of their wedding day has others counting down the days, not because of their excitement for her but instead hoping she will "chill" and get back to normal afterwards. It is this type of anticipation that Jesus is looking for in His Bride, an anticipation and longing for His return so she can spend all eternity with Him.

In John 14:2-3, Jesus tells us that He's going to go prepare a place for us in His Father's house. This is in line with what we covered in the sequence of events of the ancient Jewish marriage customs, where the groom would leave his new bride for a period to prepare a place at his father's house for them. In conjunction with this, there is a statement that Jesus makes multiple times in the Gospels relating to this very anticipation, a statement that is oftentimes overlooked or discounted for one reason or another. Yet, it is a statement closely connected with our marriage to Christ and our future wedding day. In Mark 13:33, when referring to His return for the Church, His Bride, Jesus tells us to, "watch and pray." This is because we do not know when He will return for us. Looking at the sequence of events associated with the ancient Jewish marriage customs, we saw that the groom would leave his new bride for an undetermined period to prepare a place for her. I don't know what his exact words would've been to her upon leaving, but he no doubt told her something to the effect that she needed to be both watching for him to return, and to be prepared to leave with him once he came. So, the question must be asked, what does it mean to watch, and what is it that we are to be praying about?

In Luke 21:34-36, we again read of Jesus telling His followers to watch and pray regarding His return for them, instructions that are given to us as well. In verse 36, Jesus gives us some substance about what we are to be praying. We are to pray that we're counted worthy to escape the things that are going to come to pass and to stand before Jesus.

We're to be praying that we are counted worthy to escape things? Some argue that those who believe and look for the Rapture of the church are merely embracing a theology of escapism. This is something on which they contend we as Christians shouldn't be focused. However, Jesus makes it clear that we are to pray that we are counted worthy to escape what is coming. How can one argue against something that Jesus, Himself, tells us to do? Some believe that once a person becomes a Christian, they are automatically considered worthy to be raptured up, but as we will later see, this is not the case.

What about what we are to be watching for? In the parable of the ten virgins found in Matthew 25:1-13, it is commonly understood that the ten virgins represent Christians, especially since in this parable as they are all waiting and looking forward to the return of their groom. In Matthew 25:6, we're told that a cry went out alerting the virgins of the imminent return of their groom. Similarly, I believe the cry going out for us today is the continuing and approaching fulfillment of Biblical end-time prophecies, alerting us to the imminent return of Jesus for His Bride.

When Jesus returns, it's not like we're going to see Him coming in the clouds as the world will see when He returns at the end of the Tribulation period. So, if we're not going to be able to see Him coming like the postman walking down the street, then what are we to be watching for? Jesus gave us signs to be watching for, signs of the last days pointing to the coming judgments of God upon the earth. I believe we are to be watching for the fulfillment of these signs, and since we know that the Rapture will take place before the Tribulation period, we know that the fulfillment of these signs points to His ever nearer return for His Bride. To be watching for Him means that we know this is not our home, and that we are always living with the awareness that He will be returning for us at any time.

Much can be said regarding the wise and foolish virgins represented in this parable, but the fact is that while all were watching, only five of them were ready for him. In verse 13 Jesus ends the parable by telling us that we need to be watching for His return, especially since we don't know when that will be.

Some argue that it's not imperative for us to be watching for Jesus' return. But Jesus makes an interesting statement in the Book of Revelation, which was written about 55-60 years after His ascension to heaven. In Revelation 16:15, between the sixth and seventh bowl judgments, Jesus tells us; "Behold, I am coming as a thief. Blessed is he who watches, and keeps his garments, lest he walk naked and they see his shame", (NKJV). Wow. On one hand Jesus tells those who watched and kept their garments, their robes of righteousness, that they are blessed. Yet, on the other hand He rebukes those who didn't by telling them they would be walking naked, and others would see their shame. How would they be walking naked and people see their shame? Could it be that they were Christians that neglected keeping their robes of righteousness free of sin and the filth of this world system? Could the result be that they not only got left behind at the Rapture, but that they also had their robes of righteousness taken from them? Can you imagine what others would say knowing they were professing Christians but got left behind? Can you imagine the shame these professing Christians would have for knowing but neglecting to be ready and prepared for Jesus when He returned? In Mark 13:37, Jesus doesn't mince words when He tells us with emphasis to watch. If Jesus takes watching for Him this seriously, shouldn't we do the same?

The bride is continually looking forward to the day of the wedding. She's not just living life knowing the day will soon arrive and that she'll be ready for it. She's living with the awareness and anticipation of that day, so everything she says and does is with that one thing in mind. As the Bride of Christ, we need to be watching with anticipation the return of our Groom. Have you ever sat looking out the window of your house watching for the arrival of someone you're so anxious to see that the anticipation was so great it almost made you sick, aching for that person to get there? I envision this is the way we need to be watching for Jesus. If we're not anxious about seeing Jesus return for us, doesn't that mean we're okay with life as it is? Wouldn't that mean we're comfortable enough in this world that if Jesus delayed His return we would be okay with it? This is a dangerous mindset to have. In Matthew 24:45-51 and Luke 12:42-47, Jesus makes it clear that those who think He is delaying His return, and therefore don't do what God's will for them is, will get left behind. They will be judged and given their portion among the hypocrites. They apparently were not watching and praying.

Some think that doing all the right things, embracing all the right doctrines and theologies, and living as they ought to be is good enough, but Jesus gives us a warning to be heeded here. In Revelation 2:1-7, speaking to the church of Ephesus, Jesus tells them they are doing everything right, but that He nonetheless has something against them. They left their first love, specifically their first love for Him. They were on top of things, even exposing those who presented themselves as sent from God when they were not, but somewhere down the road of life they had left their first love for Christ. Jesus makes it clear that, unless they repent and return to their first love for Him, He would remove the lampstand, His presence, from them. One of the aspects of someone's love for Jesus, a first love for Him, is their eager anticipation and longing for His return for them. Do you have that first love for Jesus, or do you need to find that again within yourself?

There's another aspect associated with the anticipation of Jesus' return we need to consider. Often, a bride will have someone help her prepare for her wedding day. That person could be a close friend or relative, or someone that they've hired for that purpose. What would you say if the bride based her relationship with her groom primarily on her relationship with her helper? In other words, what if she developed such a strong relationship with the one helping her prepare for the wedding, that she felt such a relationship was an indicator of how ready she would be for her groom? In much the same way, some consider their right standing with Christ to be based on their relationship with the Holy Spirit. In John 14:16, Jesus lets us know that He was going to pray to the Father that He will send us a helper, the Holy Spirit. We're also told in John 14:26 that the Holy Spirit will teach us all things and remind us of what He said to us. In John 15:26, Jesus tells us the Holy Spirit, our Helper, will testify of Him. Jesus tells us it's to our advantage that the Holy Spirit would come to us, but that He would have to leave before the Holy Spirit could come. The Holy Spirit is our wedding helper, the one who helps us prepare for our wedding day with Jesus.

There is a tendency for some to focus on the operation of the gifts of the Holy Spirit, or to seek supernatural experiences for themselves or for others. Whether they realize it or not, some of those whom I just described seem to base their relationship with Christ according to their relationship with the Holy Spirit. The Holy Spirit is not our groom, but instead one that is helping us be prepared for Jesus who is our groom. The Holy Spirit will not be the one that determines if we are ready when Jesus returns. Instead, it will be Jesus who will make that determination. Since when did the wedding planner determine if the bride was ready and presentable to the groom? The wedding planner can only do the best job he or she can to prepare the bride as she will allow, but it is the groom that gives his seal of approval or not. The Holy Spirit helps, teaches, convicts, comforts, and empowers us to be witnesses of Christ, but He won't be the one that determines if we have adequately prepared for the return of our Groom. In watching for our Groom's return, we must stay focused on Him, not on the One that is helping us prepare for Him. If we are focused more on our relationship with the Holy Spirit than on our relationship with Christ, we aren't watching for Him to return. The Holy Spirit will always point us to Jesus, and never towards Himself.

Be watching for Jesus, our Groom, because He can return for us at any moment. When He does, it will be the start of a glory filled future for us.

Preparation of the Bride

In the previous chapter, we looked at the anticipation of the bride for her groom's return, or more specifically the anticipation we should have for the return of Jesus for us, His Bride. We looked at the importance of watching for Jesus' return and what that looks like, but in this chapter, we're going to look at the importance of praying while we're watching for Him.

In Mark 13:32-33, Jesus tells us we don't know when He will be returning. Because we can't know, we need to watch and pray. While we can certainly understand our need to be watching for Him, why should we be praying as we watch and wait? What is Jesus trying to tell us here? In Luke 21:34-36, which again refers to the time He will return for us, Jesus gives us some direction as to what we are to be praying for while we're watching for Him. In verse 36 Jesus tells us; "Watch therefore, and *pray always that you may be counted worthy* to escape all these things that will come to pass, and to stand before the Son of Man." (NKJV) (Italics added for emphasis). Pray that we're counted worthy? Is He talking to unbelievers? Why would believers have to pray that they're counted worthy? After all, are we not automatically counted worthy at the point of salvation? To understand what the preparation of the Bride means to us, let us first take a closer look about what it means to be counted worthy.

Some would argue that these words of Jesus were spoken before his death and resurrection and therefore not relevant to us. They often take the position that once someone receives salvation there is nothing more he is to do because he is now under grace. Living by a set of rules and laws after receiving such grace is being legalistic. While it is true that Ephesians 2:8-9 makes it clear our salvation is by grace and not by works, does that mean works are not to be a part of our life as a follower of Christ? It is true that the words noted above, spoken by Jesus, came before His death and resurrection, but there are some words He said after His resurrection, and just before His ascension, we need to remember. In Matthew 28:19-20, Jesus instructs His followers to make disciples of all nations, teaching them to obey all He had commanded them. He didn't say to obey just the things He told them after He rose from the dead, but instead all that He had commanded them. It doesn't matter if all His words were based on the Law or on grace, the fact remains He left specific instructions to obey all His commands. Twice within the same chapter, John 14:15, 21, Jesus makes it clear that if a person truly loves Him he will keep and obey His commandments. This situation is further reinforced in the Book of Revelation, written about 50-60 years after Jesus ascended. In chapters 2-3 Jesus addresses seven churches. In His address to these churches, Jesus gives brief comments about each one and what about them did and did not please Him. Regarding those things that displeased Him, He gave specific instructions as to what they were to do to remain in good standing with Him. If they didn't do those things He listed, specific consequences would come that involved severing their relationship with Him. In each of these passages, it appears that Jesus has specific expectations of His followers.

In Acts 15:22-29, as a response to the conflict between Jewish and gentile Christians regarding the keeping of the law, the Jerusalem Council made a decree as to what was expected of gentile followers of Christ. In the Council's decree, it was made clear in verse 28 that the list of things they were instructing the gentile believers to abide by even pleased the Holy Spirit, further reinforcing the position that there are expectations of behavior and practice Jesus has for His followers. What is further seen in verses 6-21, is that there is nothing mentioned by the Apostles that Jewish converts were no longer expected to follow aspects of the law as a way of life. Instead it is implied that salvation is not found in the keeping of the law, but by grace. This understanding is what brought them to the conclusion that it was not for them to require gentiles to do the works of the law. However, that understanding did not negate the fact there were to be expectations that gentile followers of Christ needed to obey.

The Book of Romans is known to hold a wealth of doctrinal nuggets from which we are to learn. In Romans 1:6-7, it is made plain that this book is written to all the Christians in Rome. It didn't matter if they were Jew or gentile, rich or poor, slave or free, or even male or female. If they were a follower of Christ then Paul was writing to them. This is an important fact to remember when we look at other portions of this powerful book. In chapter 6, a chapter that focuses on being slaves of sin or slaves of righteousness, we understand that Paul is still talking to Christians. We know this because he talks of people choosing to submit themselves to righteousness, something that non-Christians are not able to do, or to sin. We are reminded in Ephesians 2:1-3, as well as in other passages, that every person is born into sin and is spiritually dead, bound to submit themselves to sin in one capacity or another. We also know that once a person receives salvation through Jesus, not only are they free from the penalty of sin, but they are also free from the bondage of sin's control over them. So, with that understanding, we can see that Paul is still addressing Christians when he tells us to not submit ourselves to sin and the flesh, since only Christians can be free to choose.

I know many who like chapter 8 because they see it as a chapter which distinguishes between Christians and non-Christians. However, Paul makes a statement in that chapter which conflicts with that argument, a statement that further reinforces the position I'm presenting. In Romans 8:13, Paul tells us that those who live according to the flesh will die. If this is a chapter distinguishing between Christians and non-Christians, then Paul should have changed his words in this verse. As I mentioned earlier, we are all born into sin and spiritually dead, and that it is only through salvation through Christ that one becomes spiritually alive. If Paul is talking to non-Christians in this verse, how can they die spiritually if they are already spiritually dead? They can't because what is already dead cannot die again. With that understanding, as in chapter 6, Christians have the choice whether to live according to the flesh or not, and if they do they will once again become slaves of sin and die spiritually.

Jesus tells us in John 8:36, that "if the Son makes you free, you shall be free indeed." (NKJV) Some look at this passage and assume that as Christians we are, and forever shall be, free from sin and its penalties. However, we need to keep this in the context in which Jesus spoke it. In response to the Jews' comments that as descendants of Abraham they have never been in bondage, found in John 8:34, Jesus makes it clear that anyone who commits sin is a slave of sin. What Jesus is telling us is that if He makes us free from the power and bondage of sin, then we are truly free. That freedom is not an illusion giving us the impression that we are free when we are not, but that we are truly free. When Jesus makes us free, He didn't remove our free will to sin again, but rather gave us the freedom to choose whether to sin or not.

The situation is like that of a person who was found guilty of being a mass murderer and sentenced to die. Suppose this same man then receives a pardon from the Governor, setting him free from prison and from ever being prosecuted for those same crimes again. However, after being freed from prison, and being free to live a good life as a law-abiding citizen, this person goes and murders more people. As a result, he is convicted and sentenced to die for the murders he committed after being pardoned. This man had the freedom to choose how to live, but he chose the wrong way. Romans 6 speaks of the freedom we have as Christians to choose to whom or to what we will become a slave. Romans 8 follows this up by telling us what the consequences will be if we choose to live in the flesh, that is, to submit once more to sin in our lives.

That consequence is to die spiritually and not be called the children of God. When Jesus makes us free, we are genuinely free to live as we choose, whether it is a life submitted to Him or to sin.

So, what does all this have to do with the preparation of the Bride of Christ? It has a lot to do with it. If we fail to realize there are expectations of us as followers of Christ, then there is no way that we can properly prepare for the return of our Groom for us, His Bride. To prepare ourselves for the return of Christ requires effort on our part. A failure to put forth the necessary effort puts us in jeopardy of not being properly prepared for Him.

Where does this preparation begin? In Romans 10:9-10, Paul tells us what is necessary for salvation, to enter this marriage relationship with Christ, but Luke tells us what Jesus says regarding His expectations of us beyond the point of salvation. The first step in our preparations for Him is found in Luke 9:23-26. Jesus tells us that our life is no longer our own to be lived as we please, but that we are to deny ourselves for Him daily. He further indicates that those who try to save their lives will lose them, but those who lose their lives for His sake will save them. Paul gives us another picture of this type of commitment to Christ in Galatians 2:20, when he tells us that he's been crucified with Christ, and that the life he now lives is Christ living within him.

In the New Testament, Jesus is referred to in three different ways, as Savior, Savior and Lord, and Lord. Savior is used more than 20 times, Savior and Lord together used more than 15 times, but Jesus is referred to as Lord over 700 times. Many have entered a relationship with Christ thinking of Him only as their savior, but as we can see in Scripture this is not enough. Jesus is to be both our Savior and Lord. To be our Lord, we must understand that we are to be obedient to Jesus in all things, even if it means doing so in areas and in ways that we don't understand, agree with, or like. To reject this type of relationship with Christ will keep one from preparing himself for His return, and subsequently not heeding Jesus' instructions to us in Luke 21:36.

Is Jesus your Lord, or have you kept Him only in the role of Savior in your life? Some may argue that there is no difference between the two, but this is not the case. Suppose you are a Game Warden out hiking around in the woods. You come across someone who has been lost for several days, someone that has slipped off a ledge and is holding onto a tree root 300' above the canyon floor. This person is calling out for help. You respond by quickly lowering a rope to pull him back up to safety. You've just saved that person. Now, let's say as the Game Warden you begin to give him instructions that he needs to follow to get to his destination safely. Despite your obvious care and concern he chooses to ignore your instructions even though he is greatly appreciative of how you just saved him. You're still his savior, but he's not letting you have any voice in his life or the decisions he will have to make. A few days later this man still hasn't arrived at his destination, so you decide to go looking for him. Starting from where you last saw him, it doesn't take long for you to find his body. Ignoring your instructions, this man thought he could safely get to his destination faster by going over a mountain of boulders, only to fall about 20' into a den of rattlesnakes. This Game Warden was his savior, but he wasn't his lord. The man was excited and very appreciative of the help he received, but he chose to not be submitted to the authority of the Game Warden, or to follow the instructions given him by the same Game Warden. Many have accepted Jesus as their savior, but this by itself will only keep them from being adequately prepared when Jesus returns for His Bride. We're told in Proverbs 14:12 that "There is a way that seems right to a man, but its end *is* the way of death." (NKJV).

What does it mean to be "counted worthy," or prepared,

when Jesus returns? Ephesians 5:27 tells us what Jesus is looking for in His Bride when He returns for her. We're told that Jesus is looking for a bride without spot or wrinkle, or any such thing, and that she should be holy and without blemish. To be holy fits in with the ancient Jewish marriage customs and what was expected of the bride. When the bride accepts the groom's proposal of marriage, she then becomes unavailable to anyone else, set apart for only her groom. At this point she changes her appearance and the way she dresses to show others publicly that she is spoken for and unavailable. Often, she would wear a veil with a headband holding some of the coins paid to her by the groom or his father. She could also include wearing some of the jewelry she received from her groom.

Some of the things the bride once did as an available virgin are no longer a part of her life. Instead, her attention is fixed on her groom. Her life is focused on getting ready for her new married life. Everything about her life is changing to reflect that she is betrothed to someone. Her life is now set apart for her new groom, and everything she does is with him in mind. During this betrothal period, the bride is preparing both her wedding garments and other apparel, blankets and linens for her new life with her groom. As one writer put it, she is preparing to be the Proverbs 31 woman for her groom and their new life together. In just the same way, Christians, as the Bride of Christ, our lives must be set apart for Him and Him alone. Everything we do must be done with Him in mind.

There is a growing trend within church circles that gives little value to being set apart for Christ in behavior and appearance. In the quest to be relevant to the world around them they think it more important to act, look, and talk like the world to reach them. It's not an issue of how much or little make-up a woman wears, or if she is or is not required to wear a dress. It's not even an issue of whether someone can go bowling or watch a movie at a theater. The real issue is, are you mindful of your Groom in all you say and do, where you go and how you dress. Are you seeking to honor and please Him first and foremost, or are you more caught up with living life as you desire and choose to do? Is your life set aside for Him and Him alone, or are you expecting Him to share the throne in your life with another person, thing or activity? Are you preparing yourself for a life of eternity with the Groom you're betrothed to, or more caught up with living the life you desire?

One of the aspects of preparing ourselves for our Groom's return ties in with making sure our garments are free of blemishes. According to the Merriam-Webster dictionary, one definition of blemish is: *a mark that makes something imperfect or less beautiful; an unwanted mark on the surface of something.* It is with this in mind that we need to ask ourselves what could create blemishes in the heart and life of a Christian. When a person surrenders his life to Christ and asks for His forgiveness of his sins, he begins his

Christian walk with a clean slate. That doesn't mean that he is perfect, but instead that he is clean and empowered to live freely and in accordance to God's will for all followers of Jesus. Some would argue that a Christian remains with a clean slate apart from anything he does or doesn't do, but if that is the case then why would the Apostle Paul make a point of how Christ's Bride is to appear when He returns for her? Unless it is possible for her to acquire some blemishes and wrinkles after salvation? More about that in the next chapter.

It is believed by some that when a person gives his or her life to Jesus, when he experiences the love God has for him, that he will never choose to hurt God or to turn away from Him. Sadly, we can read in the New Testament about how many encountered the love of Christ, yet chose to walk away from Him. Judas Iscariot is a prime example. Judas lived with Jesus for three and a half years, seeing and experiencing firsthand in his own life the love of Christ, yet his love for money, among other things, took him to the place of betraying Jesus.

Just because we gave our lives to Christ doesn't mean we lost our free will to choose whether to follow Christ or not, or that we are no longer capable of engaging in sin if that is what we want. As we stated in an earlier chapter, Romans 6 speaks to Christians about how we have the freedom to choose to submit to sin or to submit to righteousness. With the understanding that we can still sin if we choose to, even if it's disobedience to what Christ would have for us, comes the blemishes of which Paul warns. When we sin, we are putting a blemish or a wrinkle in our robes, and the only way to get those removed is to repent of that sin, to turn from it, and to ask for forgiveness. The sacrifice Jesus made on Calvary is more than sufficient to cover all our sins past, present, and future, but it can only be applied to those sins as we confess and submit them to Him for forgiveness.

In Romans 6:1, Paul asks the question, "Shall we continue in sin that grace may abound?" His response is an emphatic NO! While it is true that as Christians we may give in to sin on occasion and need to repent of it, to choose to continue in sin willfully is both wrong and dangerous as it pertains to our relationship with Christ. It doesn't matter what the sin is, no matter how small or big it may be. In finding ways to justify and rationalize the why or the how it's okay to continue in it, they are allowing the blemishes and wrinkles of that sin to remain on their robes. Our preparation for the return of our Groom includes making sure we remain clean of any sin in our life. We must understand that if we do sin then we need to take that sin and surrender it to Him as quickly as possible. 1 John 1:9 tells us that if we confess our sins, He is faithful and just to forgive us our sins. Get the sin out, and keep it out.

The Great Divorce

In the previous chapters, we covered several aspects about the betrothal stage of the ancient Jewish wedding, but in this chapter, I want to look at one aspect that is rarely mentioned. We've looked at the importance of the bride watching for the return of her groom and about her need to be prepared and ready to leave with him once he does return. But what if the groom returns to find that she's not watching for him, or that she hasn't prepared herself appropriately for him and their new life together? What if she was unfaithful in her commitment to him? Are there consequences the bride will have to face if she is guilty of the above? If so, is there something that we can learn from this regarding our own relationship with Christ?

In that day, when a bride and groom entered a marriage

covenant with each other, they were legally, socially, and religiously considered married to each other. Even though the marriage had yet to be consummated and finalized, the consequences to a violation of their marriage covenant by either one of them was serious, and at times severe. This is very different from the engagement process associated with our American wedding customs, something that can be terminated without any consequences at any given time and in the simplest of ways. In that day, if, after becoming betrothed, either one of them changed their mind, which they could do, the one who changed his or her mind would be liable for a significant fine. If the bride was found to be unfaithful, not only could the groom give her a letter of divorce, but he would also be free of paying any of the penalties outlined in their ketuba, their marriage contract, for divorcing her. We see in Scripture an example of what could happen if one of them was believed to be unfaithful to the commitment made to each other. In Matthew 1:18-19, Joseph, a just man, was looking to put Mary away privately because she was found to be with child before they consummated the marriage. Based on the culture and the nature of a betrothal, Joseph was looking to give Mary a letter of divorce, thus terminating their betrothal.

As was mentioned earlier, there were only two ways to terminate a betrothal, through divorce or death. Since we're in the betrothal stage in our marriage to Christ, is this something that we need to consider? If so, is there Scripture to support that? More importantly, what would this mean to us? Many believe once a person receives salvation, his relationship with Christ is final and irreversible, therefore it can't be terminated for any reason. For that matter, some believe if a person once appeared to have become a Christian, only to live like one no longer, then they were never saved from the start. Are these statements true, or does Scripture tell us something different?

The first question that must be asked is, would Jesus

ever divorce us? In Jeremiah 3:8, God indicates that He divorced Israel. In Isaiah 50:1, God further indicates that He gave a bill of divorce. And in Hosea 2:2, God makes it clear that Israel is not His wife. While scholars seem to disagree concerning what these passages mean, and whether they should be taken literally or not, the one thing that is true is that in these Spirit inspired passages God is using marriage terms when describing His relationship with Israel: wife, divorce, and adultery. We also read in Malachi 2:16 that God hates divorce. On top of these, in Matthew 19:3-12 and Mark 10:2-12, Jesus doesn't speak too highly of divorce, reminding the Pharisees that from the beginning divorce was not part of God's plan for marriage. So, where does all of this leave us?

When we read of the divorce God gave Israel, and His reasons for doing so, we also see that Judah was guilty of doing the same offenses as Israel, yet there is no record of Judah getting a similar divorce from God. The book of Hosea, written prior to Jeremiah and

Isaiah, gives Israel their divorce. According to David Instone Brewer in a Tyndale House bulletin, God's statement in Hosea 2:2 regarding Israel, "For she is not My wife, nor am I her husband!", was the single phrase listed on most divorce decrees among Jews in the Old Testament that officially declared the divorce. This phrase was more than likely what Jeremiah and Isaiah referred to regarding God's divorce of Israel. But, what were the reasons for the divorce? Quite simply, adultery. Israel had flirted with and engaged in the pursuit of other gods, engaging in idolatry. This amounted to nothing less than adultery with God. When Malachi spoke of divorce, looking at the context in which it was written, the treachery spoken of is the disregard for the covenant and the one with whom they were in covenant. It appears that the crux of these passages is the fact that when one devotes his or her attention and affections on someone or something other than the one to whom he or she covenanted with in marriage, unfaithfulness has occurred. Either someone was divorced because they gave the affections and devotions they promised to one to someone or something else, or in the case of Malachi, someone chose to divorce the other without just cause to pursue someone else. Even though God apparently divorced Israel, that doesn't change the fact that the Jews are still God's chosen people, and that He has a definite plan for them in these last days. Some would like to say that God is done with Israel, and that the Church took its place. But that is not the case when we remember that major components of end time events are centered around Israel coming to the place that they recognize Jesus as their Messiah, as well as the fulfillment of a kingdom that God had promised them thousands of years ago.

What does all of this have to do with us and our relationship with Christ? A lot. As we covered in previous chapters, it is our responsibility as the Bride of Christ to be watching and to be praying that we are counted worthy to leave with Him when He returns for us. What if Jesus comes back to find that we haven't been watching for Him, that we haven't taken our preparations to be ready when He returned seriously, or that we've been unfaithful in our commitment to Him? If God chose to issue a divorce decree to Israel for their adultery, how can we be so adamant that Jesus would never do the same with us?

Jesus made it very clear that we are to be watching for Him. It wasn't a casual suggestion as some would suggest, but instead a strong command that He expected us to heed. The reason we are to be watching is that we do not know when He would be returning for us. Jesus made it clear that those who are not watching for Him would be left behind. This wasn't a command Jesus gave to people who were not following Him. It was a command to His followers!

We see the gravity of Christ's command in Matthew 25:1-13, the parable of the ten virgins. In this parable, it is commonly understood that all the virgins represent Christians, those who have been made pure through

Christ. This is the case since non-Christians would not be looking for the return of Christ, our Groom. Five of the virgins were wise, and five were considered not just un-wise, but foolish. The five wise ones were prepared, but the five foolish ones were not. While the five foolish ones went to those who buy and sell in a hurried attempt to be prepared for the groom, the groom came and took the five wise virgins with him, leaving the five foolish ones behind. When the five foolish ones returned, they tried to enter in where the groom and the five wise virgins went, calling out to the groom as "Lord", but the groom denied them entrance, telling them that He did not know them. This sounds like the divorce decrees of the Old Testament and the days of Jesus, "She is not my wife, and I am not her husband". It is then that Jesus stresses to His followers the need to be watching and praying regarding His return. Both the wise and foolish virgins had been waiting for the groom's return, but only five of them made sure to maintain a state of preparedness so they would be ready no matter when he did so.

In Matthew 18:21-35, we read of another parable Jesus gave about an unforgiving servant. In this parable, the unforgiving servant represents a Christian. This is because his entire debt had been forgiven him by the king, much like our debt is to God when we receive salvation. This servant, after having been forgiven all his mountain of debt, went out and refused to forgive another one their debt to him. As a result, the king remembered this unforgiving servant's debt he had previously forgiven and sent this servant to the torturers until all his debt was paid. Considering how large it was, the debt could never be paid.

Some will argue that God will never remember what He's forgiven, citing the following passages: Psalms 103:12 which speaks of removing our sins as far from us as the east is from the west, and Micah 7:19 which speaks of throwing all our sins into the sea. While these passages are inspired by the Holy Spirit and true, we can't forget that God is all-knowing and sovereign. If He decides to remember them, He is more than capable of doing so. Because God is all-knowing, we must conclude that for Him to forget something isn't because He forgets it, but that He is choosing never to hold those sins against us. With that in mind, we must consider the point that Jesus is making in this parable, that just because the king forgave his servant all his debt didn't mean he couldn't remember it if the servant did not extend the same forgiveness and grace he received to others. This point is confirmed in Matthew 18:35 when Jesus says God, our heavenly Father, will do the same if we don't forgive. We have been forgiven much, but if we don't forgive others God will remember what we've been forgiven and hold us accountable for those sins.

For those who want to say that Jesus said these things before His death and resurrection, so that they don't apply to us now, let's look at some of what Jesus said after His resurrection. To begin with, in Matthew

28:18-20, some of the last things Jesus said to His followers before He ascended to heaven, He gives instructions to teach disciples of His to observe and obey all the things He had commanded them. Jesus didn't limit what is to be taught to only those things shared after His resurrection, but instead all that He had taught and commanded them, which would include His teachings through parables and His commands to watch and pray. The Book of Revelation was written decades after Christ ascended to heaven, according to most scholars between 81-92 A.D. In Revelation 2-3, we see Jesus addressing seven churches, churches made up of Christians. In Revelation 2:5, Jesus tells the church of Ephesus that if they don't repent He will break relationship with them. In Revelation 2:16, Jesus tells the church of Pergamos to "repent, or else …". In Revelation 2:22-23, Jesus tells the church in Thyatira that He will cast them into great tribulation unless they repent of what they've been doing. In Revelation 3:2-4, Jesus tells the church of Sardis to be watchful, and if they don't hold fast to what they've heard and received with repentance, if they will not watch, He will come upon them as a thief. Jesus also mentions to this church that those who don't repent and start watching for Him will have their names blotted out of the Book of Life (also known as the Lamb's Book of Life). In Revelation 3:16, addressing the fact that they were lukewarm, He tells the church of Laodicea that He will spit them out of His mouth.

What we just looked at are Scripture passages that indicate Christians who are not watching for Him, Christians who do not repent of and turn away from their sins, and Christians who are lukewarm in their relationship with Jesus or do not persevere, will experience a break in their relationship with Him. In other words, they will experience a divorce from Christ that will have eternal consequences. This is a very sobering thing to think about as we live each day. Are we living, saying and doing things that are honoring and pleasing in the sight of God, or are we living with continual sin in our life that we are rationalizing and justifying as being okay?

Another sobering passage is found in Matthew 7:21-23. Here we find a truth that we need to understand and embrace if we are to enter heaven. Jesus tells us that not everyone who calls Him Lord will enter the kingdom of heaven. He also tells us that it doesn't matter what is on our spiritual resume. Things that we've done in His name and in the power of the Holy Spirit, are not guarantees that we are in right relationship with Him as many would seem to think. In verse 23 Jesus responds to their claims that He is their Lord and to their impressive resume of things they've done in His name, telling them to depart from Him because He didn't know them since they were practicing lawlessness. Lawlessness? These people were calling Him Lord and doing great and mighty things in His name! Jesus told us in verse 21 that only those who do the will of the Father will enter heaven. Those He told to depart from Him were not doing the will of the Father. God can see beyond what everyone else sees in us because He knows our heart, those areas of our lives that nobody else can know. He knows if we are in disobedience, in rebellion, towards Him and His lordship in any area of our lives. As we mentioned in an earlier chapter, many people have accepted Jesus as their Savior, but they haven't accepted Him as their Lord. They are buying into the deception that once they got saved, once they entered the grace God has for us, there is nothing more that God requires of them. This is a deceptive trap that can have eternal consequences if we are not living submitted to and subject to His lordship in our lives. If we continue in disobedience to Him then we run the risk that He will divorce us, telling us to depart from Him when Jesus returns for His Bride, or when we step into eternity through death. If we repent of the rebellion, submit those areas of our lives that we had not been under His lordship to Him, turn away from the disobedience we've been rationalizing as okay in our life, then we can have confidence that our eternal home will be with Him.

When we talk of divorce, some are quick to say that the husband is always to blame as the leader in that relationship, but using that same logic one must then conclude that both God the Father and Jesus, the two most perfect of husbands, are the ones to blame in their divorces. Scripture is clear that is not the case. Instead, Scripture tells us that the blame for the Father's divorce from Israel was the idolatry and adulterous choices and decisions Israel made. Regarding the coming divorce between Jesus and some in the body of Christ, Scripture is once again clear that the blame rests squarely on the one divorced and not on Jesus. Don't think that I'm saying the blame of one's divorce is always on the wife, because I'm not. But to say that the responsibility for all divorces rests on the husband is not a true or accurate position either.

There is a great divorce coming. The main reason many will be divorced from Christ will not be based on what they did or did not do for Him, but instead on whether they were obedient to do the will of the Father in their lives. When God asks you for grapes, are you giving Him grapes, or are you giving Him apples because you want to keep the grapes for yourself? Moses, a prophet and a man of God, someone God called His friend, was denied entrance to the promised land because of disobedience. How can we as Christians then expect to enter heaven with disobedience in our heart?

The Groom Returns

The previous chapters set the stage, prepared the foundation, that leads up to the next major prophetic event. This event is closely connected to marriage, specifically our marriage to Christ. The event I'm talking about is what we commonly refer to as the Rapture. There are some who take the position that this event is not a Biblically sound interpretation of Scripture. They are so certain that they believe it is heresy to hold to such a doctrine. As we've seen in the previous chapters, our relationship with Christ is closely linked to and modeled by the ancient Jewish wedding customs, and the Rapture is clearly pictured within those same wedding customs. Based on the model we've been given in the ancient Jewish wedding customs for our relationship with Christ, should there be no Rapture then there would be no concluding wedding ceremony.

It is true that the word "rapture" is not found in most English Bibles, but on the other hand neither is "trinity" or "millennium", terms that are generally accepted as doctrinally sound. The word rapture comes from the Latin word, "rapturo", which is used to translate the Greek word "harpazo" found in 1 Thessalonians 4:17. The Greek word "harpazo" means to seize, to snatch up, or to take away by force, either spiritually or physically. In the context of 1 Thessalonians 4:17, and the corresponding scripture in 1 Corinthians 15:51-52, it is clear that "harpazo" is being used in the context of a physical, bodily removal of the followers of Christ. There are some who try to say that what the Apostle Paul is referring to in 1 Thessalonians 4:17 is a spiritual, euphoric type of experience, but a closer look at the text would indicate it is actually a literal, physical, bodily removal yet to be experienced.

The event to which we ascribe the word, rapture, is

clearly seen in Scripture and modeled in part in both the Old and New Testaments. In the Old Testament, we see both Enoch and Elijah being caught up to heaven. In the New Testament we see Philip, a disciple of Christ, twice physically caught up and instantly taken to a different location. Oh, and let us not forget that Christ was also caught up when He ascended to heaven after His resurrection.

Some believe the concept of a Rapture is a relatively new idea originating from the early 1800's, but this is not the case. We see the English word, rapture, used as early as 1748 in Dr. John Gill's commentary on 1 Thessalonians 4:1.

"The Apostle, having something new and extraordinary to deliver concerning the coming of Christ, the first resurrection, or the resurrection of the saints, or the change of the living saints, and the Rapture both of the raised, and the living in the clouds to meet Christ in the

air expresses itself in this manner." - Dr. John Gill (Baptist Theologian) in 1748

While some would argue that a pre-Tribulation rapture is also a new concept that is taught, we see two early examples in records written as early as 100-120 A.D. by the Shepherd of Hermas and in 373 A.D. by Ephraim the Syrian that would indicate that they embraced a pre-Tribulation catching up of the Church, a pre-Tribulation rapture.

"You have escaped from the great tribulation on account of your faith, and because you did not doubt in the presence of the beast ... Go, therefore, and tell the elect of the Lord His mighty deeds, and say to them that this beast is a type of the great tribulation that is coming. If ye then prepare yourselves, and repent with all your hearts, and turn to the Lord, it will be possible for you to escape it, if your heart be pure and spotless, and ye spend the rest of your lives serving the Lord

blamelessly." – The Shepherd of Hermas (100-120 A.D.)

"... All the Saints and the elect of God are gathered together before the tribulation which is about to come, and are taken to the Lord, in order that they may not see at any time the confusion that overwhelms the world because of our sins." – Ephraim the Syrian (from the Greek Orthodox Church) 373 A.D.

The idea and teaching of the Rapture, as well as a pre-Tribulation Rapture, is not as new as some claim that it is. Instead it falls in-line with what we're seeing in Scripture and with the different keys God has given to help us better understand prophetic end time events. We've seen in John 14:1-3 that Jesus, our Groom, has gone to prepare a place for us in His Father's house, and that He will be returning at some point in the future to take us back to His Father's house. We've also seen that we, as the Bride of Christ, are to be watching and preparing ourselves to be ready to leave with Him when He returns. Both aspects of our relationship with Christ have at their focus the Rapture of the Church to Christ. In 1 Thessalonians 4:13-18 and 1 Corinthians 15:50-58, we see a picture of what is going to happen at the time of the Rapture, an exciting picture at that. In 1 Thessalonians 4:16 we see Jesus coming for us from heaven, much like a groom returns for his bride. We also see in 1 Corinthians 15:52 that when Jesus comes for His Bride, she will be almost instantaneously changed from corruptible to incorruptible. This is exciting for those who are in Christ, whether they be dead or alive when He returns.

Sadly, this event isn't going to be exciting for everyone, though. One of the aspects relating to the groom's return for his bride is something we need to remember when we think of Jesus' return for His Bride. No one knew when the groom was returning, except for one person. The groom did not know when he would return. The bride did not know. None of their friends or family knew, except for the groom's father. The groom's father was the one that determined if a place was adequately prepared for his son's bride, so it was up to him to tell his son when to return for his bride. In like manner, that is exactly what we hear from Jesus. Speaking of His return for us, in Matthew 24:36 Jesus makes it clear that only the Father knows when He will be returning. Verse 42 and Matthew 25:13 emphasize that point even more, instructing us to be watching and ready when the time of His return for us comes. This is one of the reasons why we're looking for a pre-Tribulation Rapture. Jesus continually tells us to be watching and ready for the time when He returns, making it clear that it could be at any given moment, with no pre-conditions. However, to take a position that the Rapture will either be mid-tribulation, pre-wrath, or even post-tribulation, among others, gives one the false security that there is still more time before His return, and that it narrows the window in which they believe Christ will return. As a result, the trap that is laid for those who don't believe in a pre-Tribulation Rapture is that they will lower their guard in their relationship with Christ and their readiness for Him when He returns. That is not good because they run the risk of being left behind if they are negligent to watch and prepare for Him as He has commanded us to do.

The Apostle Peter tells us in 2 Peter 3:3-9, that in the last days there will be scoffers who are skeptical that Jesus will be returning as promised. While it may seem safe to say that Peter is writing about non-believers in this passage, we have two accounts in the Gospels of Jesus speaking about followers of His that think He's delaying His return, Matthew 24:45-51 and Luke 12:35-48. In both passages, Jesus is giving a parable about a faithful and an evil servant. In these parables, the master represents Jesus, while both the faithful and the evil servants represents Christians, people who consider Jesus to be their master and expect Him to return at some time. Jesus tells us in both parables that the evil servant thought that his master was delaying his return, and because of this he lived as he pleased with no concern of consequences for his actions. However,

Jesus tells us the consequences of such a way of thinking have severe and eternal results. It was in believing the master was delaying his return, and that he didn't have to be mindful of the way he was living, that made this servant evil.

In a similar way, more and more Christians are taking the position that Jesus isn't coming soon, that it will still be many years if not decades before He returns. Some of them believe that certain events need to take place first, like a great coming revival. They believe that until such an event happens Jesus won't be coming back. This is a very deceptive trap, as we can see in these parables Jesus gave us. Scripture is very clear that we are to be expecting Jesus to return at any moment. If we are thinking that He won't return until certain conditions or events take place, then we are setting ourselves up to be the evil servants portrayed in these parables.

The Rapture of the Church we've been talking about is a marriage based event. It is exclusive to those who have received salvation, that have been watching for His return, that have been praying they are counted worthy to be received, and have prepared themselves appropriately for when that time comes. Some Christians take the position that there is no Rapture to take place, even that it's heretical to believe such a teaching. It is for this reason they probably will not be caught up to meet the Lord in the air.

Let me present one last example. After leaving Egypt, when the children of Israel prepared to enter the Promised Land the first time, they were denied access to it by God because of their unbelief. If someone doesn't believe in a future physical rapture of the Church, how can he expect to be caught up if he is wrong? Such logic doesn't make any sense, especially considering Scripture.

Other Christians believe in the Rapture and that it will take place sometime soon, but they deny the fact that the Church is the Bride of Christ. Some of them have taken the position that the Bride of Christ is the New Jerusalem, or some other person or inanimate object, despite the many passages of Scripture we've seen that dispute that. Since the Rapture is strictly an event in the marriage process between Christ and His Bride, I can't help but wonder if those who believe in a Rapture, but not in the Church being the Bride of Christ, will be left behind because they are disqualifying themselves as the Bride of Christ for which the Rapture is exclusively provided?

A minister, one of the top leaders of a religious organization that mentors and oversees churches and ministers throughout America and around the world, is so opposed to teachings in favor of the Rapture, that not only did he write a book trying to glorify being "left behind" and to attack teachings on the Rapture, but he also took the position that anyone who believes in the

Rapture is a heretic. He believes that the Rapture teaching is fear based, and therefore is not and cannot be of God. Well, the only ones who should be legitimately fearful of the Rapture are those who are not Christians, and those who are Christians who are not living in a way that is honoring and pleasing to God. For Christians who actively seek to please and honor God in all aspects of their lives, the Blessed Hope is a very exciting hope for them.

The Groom is returning, and His return is very, very close. That is extremely exciting! When He comes, life as we know it will no longer exist because we who are counted worthy (Jesus' words, Luke 21:36) will be instantly changed for an eternity with Christ. Oh, how exciting that will be!

Are you excited? If you're not, then it's time to get excited. Grab that first love you had when you first gave your life to Jesus. Be consumed with Jesus as the ever-consumed bride is over her groom. Eagerly anticipate and look forward to seeing Him face to face when He returns. Maybe your lack of excitement for the return of Christ for His Bride is because you haven't given your life to Jesus? Or, maybe it's because you did at some point in the past, but you haven't been living as you know you should be? Well, it's time to surrender your life to Jesus, to repent of and turn away from the sin in your life, and to embrace the fact that He desires to come and receive YOU unto Himself on that blessed day!!!

The Groom is returning! Are you ready????

A Sobering Thought

I've heard it said by some that if they were left behind at the Rapture of the Church they would have another opportunity to enter heaven in the Tribulation period. I don't understand why they would be so nonchalant about missing the Rapture, especially when we read of how bad things are going to get during the Tribulation period. During that time people will have to give their lives for Christ to enter Heaven. As scary as it would be to miss the Rapture and to face the wrath of God while literally and physically being required to give your life for Jesus, there's another thought that is even scarier.

In this chapter, I'm going to tackle something that you probably haven't heard before. It's something that should cause you to stop and re-evaluate things in your life a bit more closely, though if it doesn't, it should. I know for myself I would have never considered such a thought, and I venture to say it never crossed your mind, too.

Several years ago, a question crossed my mind that made me think twice about what I believed and why I believed it. We know that when the Rapture takes place, those who are dead in Christ, along with those who are alive in Christ, will be caught up to meet Jesus in the air. We also know there will be people getting saved in the Tribulation period. Because they accept and acknowledge Christ, many will literally give their lives for the sake of Jesus and the Gospel. The question that crossed my mind several years ago, simple and to the point, is whether Christians that missed the Rapture could still find their eternal destination in Heaven. It's been assumed within church circles that if a Christian missed the Rapture he would still have another opportunity to make it to Heaven, but is that what Scripture teaches us? Or, is that something we've assumed because of God's grace and mercy, giving us license to continue in sin or living contrary to the will of God if we so choose? To think that there may be no more opportunity for a Christian who neglected his relationship with Jesus, or treated it so nonchalantly that he missed the Rapture, is a very sobering thought, to say the least. Let's look and see what the Bible teaches in this regard.

I would have to say that the following passage is a scary one, perhaps one of the scariest within Scripture. I've heard some say this passage is not saying it is possible for someone to fall away in their relationship with Christ, but instead what would happen if that were a possibility. For me, I've struggled with the Scripture because it sounds scary and final, yet at the same time I've seen people who have genuinely received salvation who backslid in their relationship with Christ, and who later returned to good and right standing with Christ through repentance of sin and submission to Him. Backslidden Christians returning to right standing with

Christ is impossible when considering this passage, but we see it happen repeatedly. How can that be? Or, are we missing something that would clear things up with our understanding with this passage? What is this scary passage to which I'm referring to? It is Hebrews 6:4-6.

"For it is impossible for those who were once enlightened, and have tasted the heavenly gift, and have become partakers of the Holy Spirit, and have tasted the good word of God and the powers of the age to come, if they fall away, to renew them again to repentance, since they crucify again for themselves the Son of God, and put Him to an open shame." Hebrews 6:4-6 (NKJV)

Before I tell you what I believe is the key to understanding this passage, let's first look at another Scripture. In Matthew 25:11-12 we read the parable of the ten virgins, and of the five foolish virgins that missed the groom's return. What we read is that after the groom takes the five wise virgins back home with him, the five foolish ones who missed him go knocking on the door seeking to enter in, but were denied both entrance and relationship with the groom. They were given no alternative way to gain entrance. As we mentioned in an earlier chapter, all ten of these virgins represent Christians, both the wise and the foolish. All ten of them responded to the groom's proposal of marriage, anticipated his return by looking forward to the wedding festivities, and considered the groom to be their Lord. Yet, five were foolish in that they didn't maintain a level of preparedness, even though they did not know when the groom would return. There are Christians who are neglecting their relationship with Christ, not taking seriously the presence of sin in their lives, or consistently counting and paying the cost for following Him. As a result, they are running a big risk of being considered foolish and being left behind. In looking at the groom's response to the five foolish virgins seeking an open door, we must ask if this is what the writer of Hebrews was thinking when he penned the words found in chapter 6:4-6?

I believe the answer to understanding this passage and how backslidden Christians can return to right standing with Christ is found in the ancient Jewish marriage customs. It's something we've already covered in some detail in a previous chapter, but we didn't examine it in the context of what we are currently looking at in this chapter. The answer is in the betrothal. In 2 Corinthians 11:2 the Apostle Paul tells us that we are betrothed to Christ, a stage in the marriage process which describes our current relationship with Him. As we mentioned earlier, a betrothal is only terminated by divorce or death. As Christians betrothed to Christ, we will only see our marriage to Christ terminated if Christ returns and finds us unfaithful and foolish, or if prior to His return we die and are found to have been unfaithful and foolish in our relationship with Him. Since Christ hasn't returned for His Bride yet in what we know to be the Rapture, and since you're reading this, it's safe to say you're still alive. If you haven't been living right or taking your relationship with Jesus as seriously as you ought, now is the time to start.

In Revelation 16:15, Jesus interrupts the Apostle John's account of the bowl judgments with some very important words. Jesus said,

> *"Behold, I am coming as a thief. Blessed is he who watches, and keeps his garments, lest he walk naked and they see his shame." Revelation 16:15 (NKJV)*

Apparently, things are going to be so bad during the Tribulation period that Jesus wants to jump in and emphasize the need to be watching for Him. At first sight, it might appear that Jesus is talking to non-Christians, but this is not the case. Christians who are watching for Jesus, those who are taking care of their garments of righteousness, will not have to endure the Tribulation period. Those Christians who were not watching, who were not taking their relationship with

Jesus seriously enough to live in ways that honor Him and be free from sin, will be left behind without their robes of righteousness. Others will see their shame, shame for knowing the truth but being so foolish not to heed it as they ought.

The parable of the wedding feast found in Matthew 22:1-14 has puzzled me over the years, namely verses 11-13. In this passage, the king enters the wedding hall to find a guest there who is without a wedding garment. The king asks how it is that he entered in without it, to which the guest was speechless. I've often wondered how it is that this person could enter through the gates and onto the premises, get all the way to the wedding hall, only to arrive inside without wearing a wedding garment. The only thing that comes to mind is that the person may have been a Christian who neglected, or was foolish, in his relationship with Jesus, and as a result was left behind when Jesus came for His Bride. Knowing that only those who literally give their lives for Jesus during the Tribulation period will enter heaven, it is possible he considered another option since he squandered his relationship with Christ the first time. The guest in the parable represents this kind of person. But, as we see in Hebrews, once someone has had a relationship with Christ but fell away, it is impossible for him to receive salvation again since he would be crucifying Christ all over again.

All of this begs the question. Is there anything in your life that you consider so important that you're willing to risk losing your eternal place in heaven for it? Could that thing be a career or business opportunity? Is your education, and what it can get you, more important? What about relationships with others, family or friends? Is it the social scene, both face-to-face or online? How about recreation or entertainment? These are some of the obvious things people look at when answering that question, but what about the seemingly insignificant ones? Maybe it's allowing "pet sins" to continue and become valuable parts of your life: sins of sensuality and sexual immorality, gossip and backbiting, "white lies" and dishonest business practices, spiritual cowardice, anger and rage, idolizing celebrities and famous personalities, the excessive indulgence of various pleasures outside Godly parameters, or any other kind of "pet sin" of which you can think. If you, as a Christian, get left behind at the time of the Rapture, will you be satisfied that those things you embraced or allowed in your life now were worth eternally missing heaven for? Just something to think about.

At the Father's House

The Rapture of the Church, the Bride of Christ, is perhaps the most exciting event yet to be fulfilled for followers of Christ. For some it is the ticket to a better life, free of the hurt and pain of this life. For others, it is the moment they will finally get to see Jesus face-to-face. Still others are just looking at it as an escape from the Tribulation and the wrath of God that will be coming upon this earth. Whatever the reasons, the Rapture, that is, the catching up of the body and the Bride of Christ, is something to which Christians look forward.

It's not the Rapture itself that Christians look forward to, per se, but instead the fact that the Rapture is the gateway to a new and better life. It is the entrance into time eternal, that point in time in which we exchange these bodies in which we currently dwell for perfect and glorious ones that will never decay. It is the long-awaited arrival at the Father's house. The Rapture is the event that leads us into a glorious existence this world will never come close to offering us.

In ancient times, the bride anxiously waited for her groom to return to receive her to himself, and then to be taken back to the groom's father's house. In John 14:1-4, Jesus tells us the same thing the groom would tell his new bride.

> *"Let not your heart be troubled, you believe in God, believe also in Me.*
> *In My Father's house are many mansions, if it were not so, I would have told you. I go to prepare a place for you.*
> *And if I go and prepare a place for you, I will come again and receive you to Myself; that where I am, there you may be also.*

And where I go you know, and the way you know."
John 14:1-4 (NKJV)

The Rapture of the Church is much more than just meeting Jesus in the air. It is the point in time at which Jesus returns to receive us to Himself. Then He will immediately take us back to the Father's house where we will forever be with Him. As it was in ancient times, to be at the Father's house is to be where the marriage is at last made complete and final. It's a time filled with joy, feasting, and celebration of marriage. For those of us who are Raptured, caught up to meet the Lord in the air, it will be an event greater than anything we could ever imagine. In 1 Corinthians 2:9, we are told,

"Eye has not seen, nor ear heard, nor have entered into the heart of man the things which God has prepared for those who love Him." – 1 Corinthians 2:9 (NKJV)

In Matthew 16:27, Jesus tells us that when He returns for us He will reward each of us according to our works. The Apostle Paul, writing about these same rewards in 1 Corinthians 3:10-15, tells us that the rewards we will receive according to our works will be determined by fire. The fire will reveal whether the works we did were done with the right attitudes and motives, but if the fire reveals what we did was not with the right attitudes and motives, at least we would "be saved, yet as through fire." (1 Corinthians 3:15, NJKV)

There are differing views among scholars as to whether the Rapture is found in the Book of Revelation, and if so, where it is seen in relation to the other events that are revealed to us there. I believe the Rapture can be seen in Revelation, more specifically in Revelation 4:1 when the Apostle John is "called up" to heaven. In the previous chapters Jesus has been talking to seven churches. Chapter 3 is the last time the church is specifically mentioned on earth.

In Revelation 4:2-11, after John has been called up, we have a scene in heaven. In verse four we read of twenty-four elders sitting on thrones arranged around the throne of God. There is a lot of speculation as to who they are, and who they are not. Some believe they are strictly heavenly beings, like the four living creatures and angels. Some believe they are Old Testament saints, which would include the twelve sons of Jacob. Some believe they are the twelve sons of Jacob and the twelve apostles. Others believe they are twenty-four Raptured elders of the New Testament church, which would include the apostles. One of the reasons some believe, as I do, that these are Raptured Christians is found in Revelation 5. Here is where the Lamb, Jesus, takes the scroll from the Father and begins to break the seven seals that seal the scroll. In Revelation 5:9-10, the twenty-four elders sing a song, the words of which seem to indicate they are Raptured Christians,

"And they sang a new song, saying: You are worthy to take the scroll, and to open its seals; for You were slain, and have redeemed us to God by Your blood out of every tribe and tongue and people and nation,

And have made us kings and priests to our God; and we shall reign on the earth." – Revelation 5:9-10 (NKJV)

After Jesus takes the scroll in Revelation 5, the next few chapters reveal the significance of the seven seals He breaks to open the scroll. These seals bring judgment upon the earth. There is little argument that the judgments being poured out on the earth during this time are going to be nothing short of terrifying. In Isaiah 26:20-21 we have a passage that could very well be pointing to this time of tribulation.

"Come, my people, enter your chambers, and shut your doors behind you, hide yourself, as it were, for a little

moment, until the indignation is past.

For behold, the Lord comes out of His place to punish the inhabitants of the earth for their iniquity; the earth will also disclose her blood, and will no more cover her slain." – Isaiah 26:20-21 (NKJV)

At the time of the Rapture we are caught up to meet Jesus in the air, then ushered directly into the Father's house. In the parable of the ten virgins in Matthew 25:1-13, the five foolish virgins missed the groom's arrival. They then attempt to join in with the others, only to be turned away at the door. This would indicate that once we arrive at the Father's house a door will be shut, preventing those outside from entering. The only time we read of Jesus pouring out His wrath and judgments upon the earth is during the Tribulation period. Based on the words of Isaiah we will be both removed from the earth and taken to heaven. We will be protected and hidden from His wrath during that time, which is another reason to believe that the

Church, the Bride of Christ, will not be on earth during the Tribulation period. Instead we'll be in the Father's house.

To be in the Father's house is not only a time of new life and bodies, the distribution of rewards for what we did for Him while here, or even a time of celebration and feasting during the finalizing of the marriage process, it is also a place of protection from the wrath and judgments God is going to pour out onto the earth. It's often said that the safest place to be is in the will of God. This is even more the case than at any other time since it is God's will for every one of us to join Him in heaven.

The safest place to be during the Tribulation period is in the Father's house. Do you want to be where it's safe, where there is protection, and a whole lot of joy and celebrations? It is up to you whether or not you're going to be there.

The Grand Appearing

Keeping in line with the key we find in the ancient Jewish marriage customs, we now come to what I will call the Grand Appearing. It is another major prophetic event that is connected to our marriage relationship with Christ. The Grand Appearing is what is commonly referred to as Christ's Second Coming, an event some have mistakenly believed to be the same as the Rapture. As we will see in this chapter, these are two completely different events. In addition, there is an element to this second coming of Christ which falls in line with the key we've been looking at, further reinforcing the marriage connection between Christ and the Church. We'll look at that as well.

To begin with, let's look at the differences between the Rapture and the Second Coming of Christ. In 1

Thessalonians 4:16-17, we see that at the Rapture believers meeting Jesus in the air. However, at the time of the Second Coming we read in Revelation 19:14 that believers return to earth with Jesus. At the time of the Rapture, we read in 1 Thessalonians 4:16-17 that Jesus, Himself, removes His followers from the earth. But in Matthew 13:36-42 and 47-50 we read that at the time of the Second Coming of Christ angels go forth to remove the wicked from the earth for judgment. We further read in 1 Thessalonians 1:10 and 5:9 that the Rapture will take place prior to the Tribulation period, which is made up of God's wrath and judgments. In Revelation 19:11-16 we read of Jesus returning at the end of the Tribulation period.

As we pointed out in previous chapters, Scripture is clear we are to be looking for the Rapture to happen at any given moment. This situation is very different from what Scripture tells us of the Second Coming of Christ. There are no signs given in Scripture to indicate when the Rapture is going to take place. However, regarding the Second Coming of Christ we have many signs which point to when it will take place. The main sign leading up to the Second Coming of Christ is found in Daniel 9:27, in which we learn that a period of seven years will start after the anti-Christ confirms a seven-year covenant with Israel. This covenant, that some believe is described in Isaiah 28:14-15, marks the start of the Tribulation period.

Another difference between the two events is around judgment. With the Rapture, there is no mention of an immediate judgment. But we're told in Revelation 20:4 that at the Second Coming the judgment of the wicked takes place. We see that the Rapture is followed with seven years of wickedness on the earth that God will judge, but the Second Coming of Christ will usher in the millennial (1000-year) reign of Christ on earth.

Other differences become apparent upon further comparison. At the Rapture, a resurrection of the dead takes place prior to the catching up of those alive in Christ. But at the Second Coming of Christ a resurrection of the dead occurs after Jesus descends onto earth. We also see in 1 Corinthians 15:51-55 that at the Rapture the bodies of those in Christ, both the dead and the living, are transformed into glorified bodies. However, at the Second Coming of Christ there is no mention of a bodily transformation of any kind. Unlike the Second Coming, when Revelation 1:7 tells us all the world will see Jesus coming, the Rapture of the Church will take place in secret and instantaneously.

So, it appears from Scripture that the Rapture and the Second Coming are two very different events, which completely lines up with the key we've been looking at for understanding end-time events. Just as it was with the ancient Jewish wedding customs, Jesus returns for His Bride at the Rapture of the Church. Later Jesus and the Church, the Bride of Christ, both return to be seen publicly by all. That's right. When Jesus returns at the

Second Coming, when everyone will see Him return, His Bride, the Church will be returning with Him.

Towards the end of the Tribulation period, in Revelation 19:6-10 we see in heaven the completion of Jesus' marriage to the Church, His Bride. Following this scene, in Revelation 19:11-13 we read of heaven being opened. Jesus is on the verge of returning to do battle with the anti-Christ and the false prophet for the final confrontation that ends the Tribulation period. Then in Revelation 19:14, as Jesus is heading to battle, we read of armies in heaven, clothed in fine linen, white and clean, following Jesus on white horses. These armies are the Bride of Christ. This is in line with the ancient Jewish marriage customs. After the bride is taken by the groom back to his father's house, there would be a time of celebrating the marriage and its completion for around a week. After the celebrating and feasting, the bride and groom would return to be seen publicly for the first time as husband and wife, something that we see taking place in Revelation 19:6-

16. Further support for this idea is found in 1 Thessalonians 4:17. The Apostle Paul tells us that once we're caught up to be with the Lord at the Rapture, we will forever be with Him, which means we will be returning with Him at the end of the Tribulation period.

What we see following the return is found beginning in Revelation 20:1-3. There we read that an angel binds up Satan and casts him into the bottomless pit for 1000 years. In Revelation 20:4, we then read that thrones are established, and that "they" sat on them, and that judgment was committed to them. Some would say that the "they" mentioned in this passage are the twenty-four elders spoken of in other passages in Revelation. However, we don't see them coming back with Jesus at the end of the Tribulation period, or even being mentioned in the above verses. If we were to keep things in context with previous passages, then I believe that the "they" in this passage is the Bride of Christ, the Lamb's wife. In Revelation 1:6 we're told that Jesus has made us to be kings and priests. In addition, the

Apostle Paul tells us in 2 Timothy 2:12 that if we will endure, we will also reign with Him. Those who endured, the Bride, are the "they" that will rule and reign with Him for 1000 years, along with those who were beheaded for their witness for Jesus and for the Word of God during the Tribulation period. As Jesus reigns for 1000 years, so too will we also reign with Him. The Bride of Christ will take her place on thrones alongside her King.

I have heard some say that the Church is not the Bride of Christ. Those who disagree say that the Bride of Christ is instead the New Jerusalem. The main reason some take this position is found in Revelation 21:2, 9. In verse 2 we are told that the New Jerusalem is prepared as a bride, adorned for her husband. This is followed in verse 9, in which one of the angels tells John to "Come, I will show you the bride, the Lamb's wife." Immediately after this John is shown the New Jerusalem descending out of heaven from God.

To say that the New Jerusalem is the Bride of Christ is inconsistent with the rest of Scripture, as we have seen in previous chapters. Nowhere in Scripture are we given any indication that Jesus is betrothed to or marrying an inanimate object, including this great city of God. Instead, we continually see Scripture pointing to the Church as the Bride of Christ. Some have argued that the body of Christ cannot be the Bride, citing that the Church cannot be both the body and the Bride of Christ at the same time. However, this is very possible when considering Scripture itself. Way back in Genesis 2:24, and in many other passages throughout the Bible, we read that in marriage a husband and wife shall become one flesh. Not only was woman taken from man, but also it is in marriage the two become one flesh. From this perspective, it is very possible for the body of Christ also to be the Bride of Christ.

Another thing to take note of in Revelation 21:2 is that

the New Jerusalem is prepared AS a bride, not that it is the bride. Brides go to great lengths to prepare themselves for their husbands, and as such God has gone to great lengths to prepare His holy city, within which the Bride of Christ will dwell. So, when John is called to go see the Bride, the Lamb's wife, it's not that the New Jerusalem is the bride of Christ, but instead that the Bride of Christ are the inhabitants of the New Jerusalem which is descending from God. What a truly awesome experience that will be!

Are you looking forward to that experience? Are you setting your sights on eternity with Jesus? Are you looking forward to having gloriously transformed bodies, to be ruling and reigning with Christ? Are you anticipating inhabiting the great city of our God with Him for all eternity? There is nothing on earth that can come close to matching the splendor and grandeur awaiting those who are found to be faithful and in Christ. Your future is truly a glory filled future if you are found faithful in Christ.

What's the Point?

In the previous chapters we've looked at one of the keys God has given us to understand yet to be fulfilled end-time events, specifically that of the ancient Jewish marriage customs. We've seen in Scripture how that our relationship with Jesus is one of marriage, with Jesus being the groom and the Church being the Bride of Christ. Understanding the ancient Jewish marriage customs, and how tightly intertwined they are with end time events, gives us insight regarding our relationship with Christ and its status, as well as what awaits us in the future. When we view Scripture in the light of our marriage relationship with Jesus, as modeled in the ancient Jewish marriage customs, we begin to see Scripture in a new light. We gain a better understanding of what Jesus was trying to tell us.

We have now looked at one of the most powerful keys found in Scripture, written to help us gain understanding of future end time events. But what's the point? Why write, or read, this book? Is it merely to help us understand end time events, or what our relationship with Christ is all about? The point of this book is very simple. Jesus is coming back at any time, perhaps before you even finish reading this chapter, and it is vitally important that He find you watching and prepared for Him when He does. Many think that once they have said a prayer asking Jesus into their lives, or merely confessing that they believe He is the Son of God who died for them, their entrance into heaven is automatic and can't be nullified. However, we now know there is more to the Christian life and being ready for eternity with Him than this. If you are a Christian and thought you could figuratively skate right into heaven simply because you accepted the salvation Jesus made available to you, think again. If you think simple assent or acceptance leaves nothing more to be expected of you after entering this saving relationship with Christ, think again. The point of this book is to challenge you to re-evaluate what you believe and why, as well as to see if you are ready for Jesus when He returns for His Bride.

Perhaps you are one of those who accepted Jesus' love and forgiveness of sins, the salvation He makes available to everyone, but there are areas of your life you have not surrendered to His Lordship. You are allowing sin, things that do not honor or please God, to be a part of your life. If this is you, the point of this book is to help you realize how vitally important it is that you deal with those sins in your life. The only way to do that is to ask God's forgiveness of the sin and to turn away from it actively. You don't want to risk missing heaven because you refused to deal with sin in your life, chose to continue in things that do not honor or please God, or those things that misrepresents the heart, nature and holiness of God to those we encounter.

In Philippians 2:12 the Apostle Paul tells us, Christians, to "work out our salvation with fear and trembling." This doesn't mean that we need to be fearful, but rather to take our salvation seriously so as not to neglect or be careless with it. The Apostle Peter, in 1 Peter 5:8, further tells us, Christians, that we need to be sober and vigilant, knowing that the devil is seeking who among us he can devour and destroy. We need to take our relationship with Christ seriously, watching and preparing ourselves as a bride does, in anticipation of His return for us at the Rapture. A bride who isn't watching for her groom, or preparing herself for him, or seeking to do what she can to honor and please him, is a bride who doesn't really and truly love her groom. A bride who watches for her groom's return, who prepares herself for him, and who seeks to honor and please him in all her ways, is a bride that truly loves her groom and desires to be with him.

There is a tremendous risk for Christians who are left behind at the Rapture of the Church, a risk that eternity in heaven will no longer be made available to them. As we saw in a previous chapter, there is a very distinct possibility that those Christians who get left behind because they were not watching or prepared for Him, or because they chose to continue in sin, will find that salvation will no longer be an option for them. Knowing that this is a very real possibility should compel Christians to be diligent in their relationship with Christ. There can be no "stinkin' thinkin'", that is, sin. First priority should be making sure there is nothing that could potentially cause them to be left behind.

It's possible that the title of this book caught your attention, but you have never entered the marriage covenant relationship with Christ about which the Bible tells us. The point of this book is to alert you to what is coming, giving you an opportunity to partake in the splendor and glory awaiting those who are caught up to meet Jesus in the air. Are you interested in having a saving relationship with Jesus? If so, it's simple. To enter this relationship with Christ, you need to realize you are a sinner, eternally lost without Him. It is important to understand, and believe, that Jesus is the only begotten Son of God, and that He died on a cross to pay the penalty for your sins, as well as mine and everybody else's. Knowing this, you need to surrender your life to Jesus. That means you must ask Him to forgive you of all your sins, and make Him both Lord and Savior of your life. After entering this relationship with Christ, you must also understand that your life is no longer your own to live as you please, but that it belongs to Jesus, to be lived as He wills. Because of entering a saving relationship with Jesus, and living your life in a way that honors and pleases Him according to His will, you will be in position to be counted among those caught up to meet Him in the air to be with Him in heaven forever.

There are no formal words to say to become a Christian, a follower of Christ. In your own words, you need to say and believe in your heart the things I just shared with you. There is nothing you could have said or done, no matter how often or frequently, that can disqualify you from having relationship with Christ. Jesus wants a relationship with you. His grace, His mercy, His love, and His forgiveness are more than enough to welcome you into the family of God, no matter what is in your past or what others may say about you. Talk to Jesus right now, asking Him for forgiveness and making Him Lord of your life, then tell others of the awesome decision you just made, and the glorious future that awaits you.

In case you find it hard to know what to say to Jesus, let me give you a simple prayer you can pray to enter a saving relationship with Christ. It's not meant to be a formula of words to generate specific results, but merely a guide to help you communicate with Jesus from your heart.

Dear Jesus, I admit that I am a sinner. I know that you

died so that I could be forgiven of my sins, and I ask that you forgive me. I know that you were raised from the dead, and as a result I can have a relationship with you for all eternity. I understand that salvation is a free gift from you that I can't earn or deserve, and that it gives me the opportunity to live freely in a way that honors and pleases you. Thank you for salvation, and be Savior and Lord of my life, helping me each day to live for you. Amen.

What's the point of this book? Hopefully it is to play a part in helping you be ready for Him when He returns for His Bride. That's the point of this book.

Thank you for allowing me to speak into your life through this book. I trust it has blessed you as much as it has blessed me to write it. Thank you.

About the Author

John and his wife, Bonnie, currently live in southwest New Mexico. They have four children and one grandson. John and Bonnie have been involved in ministry over the years in various capacities. In recent years, John has been a blog writer, a Twitter Bible chat facilitator, a home group leader, and an adult Sunday School teacher, just to name a few.

More than twenty-five years ago, God birthed within John the Resounding Shophar ministry. The heart of Resounding Shophar is to remind Christians that Jesus could return at any moment, and that they need to make sure they are ready when He does return. Are you ready if Jesus were to return within the next few minutes?

You can contact the author at:

Email: pastorjohn@resoundingshophar.com
Twitter: https://twitter.com/rshophar
Facebook: https://www.facebook.com/rshophar
Website: http://resoundingshophar.com

www.ingramcontent.com/pod-product-compliance
Lightning Source LLC
Chambersburg PA
CBHW050540300426
44113CB00012B/2199